STRAIN YOUR BRAIN

BRAIN

IDEAS FOR CREATIVE

WRITTEN BY BECKY & CHARLIE DANIEL
ILLUSTRATED BY BEV ARMSTRONG

THE LEARNING WORKS

P.O. Box 6187 Santa Barbara, CA 93160

The purchase of this book entitles the
individual teacher to reproduce copies for use
in the classroom.

The reproduction of any part for an entire
school or school system or for commercial
use is strictly prohibited.

TABLE OF CONTENTS

EXAGGERATION

Exaggeration is a way of saying that something is greater or worse or better than it really is. For example: "I almost died laughing," or "Don't blow your top." Think of four or five exaggerated expressions. Write them down and draw a sketch to illustrate your statements.

ADAGES

An adage is an old saying or an expression of wisdom that people have used for many years.   For example: "Two heads are better than one," or "A leopard cannot change his spots," or "A penny saved is a penny earned." Make up your own expressions. Tell what each one means. Perhaps someday it will be an adage.

GRAFFITI

Scribbling graffiti on walls, such as "John loves Mary," or "Georgetown High '85," has been a popular pastime for many years. However, destroying public or private property is not a good way to express how one feels. Pretend you are allowed to write some graffiti on the walls of the following places. What will you write?

The White House _____
_____

The principal's office _____
_____

A local prison _____
_____

A classroom blackboard _____
_____

A hospital _____
_____

A movie theater _____
_____

Your local newspaper _____
_____

A wedding chapel _____
_____

A courthouse _____
_____

A bank _____
_____

Your living room _____
_____

Attention all astronauts: you are hereby under arrest for breaking the law _ of gravity!

A GOOD CAUSE

Choose a cause that you feel is important and that you have strong feelings about, such as saving the whales or helping poor refugees. Draw a cartoon that expresses your feelings. Then write the meaning of your cartoon in words.

COLLAGE YOURSELF

Cut pictures and words from magazines or newspapers and paste them on a large sheet of cardboard. Choose your pictures and words carefully because you want the result to be all about **you**! If you have trouble getting started, think of things you like or dislike, places you'd like to visit, foods you enjoy eating, words that describe you, etc.

PICTURE WRITING

Some Indian tribes used picture writing. You may have seen examples of this used as patterns on rugs, blankets, or pottery. Make up a picture language of your own. Write a story using your new symbols. Let a friend read your picture story. Then ask your friend to tell you the story. Did you get your meaning across? What could you have done to make your new language more accurate?

ADS THAT SELL

Cut an ad from a magazine or newspaper. Tape it to the back of this sheet. Study it carefully and answer the following questions:

1. When you look at the ad, what is the first thing that comes to your mind?

2. What do you like about the ad?

3. What do you dislike about the ad?

4. Do you think the ad is effective (does it make you want to buy the product)?

5. Who is the ad written for (age level, male or female)?

6. If you were writing the ad, how would you change it?

SLOGAN TIME

Pretend you are the campaign manager for a presidential candidate. Write a slogan and a plan for your campaign. Include a list of qualifications and personality traits that are very favorable for your candidate. Remember, you are responsible for creating your candidate's "image."

TIME FOR CAMP

Write a brochure advertising a summer camp you would like to attend. Remember it must be an ad that will appeal to your parents, who usually pay the camp fees. Describe the features of a camp that you think are desirable in a way that would interest your parents, and provide some illustrations of what the camp looks like.

EQUESTRIAN CAMP IN THE HIGH SIERRA
FOR GIRLS 12-18

Name _____

YOUR OWN BUSINESS

Pretend you are opening your own business. Design your own business cards, business sign, and your ad for the Yellow Pages. Be sure you give important information about what kind of business it is, your location, and any special features that would make your business more attractive than other similar ones. *You are a guest on Good Morning America*

WALKADOG
DOG EXERCISE SERVICE

ROBIN JOHNSON
214 CHESTNUT CIRCLE · ROXBURY, IL · 31281
(417) 218-3491

214 CHESTNUT CIRCLE
☺ HOME OF ☺
WALKADOG
DOG EXERCISE SERVICE

ROBIN JOHNSON

FRIENDLY SERVICE · REASONABLE RATES
INQUIRE WITHIN

"THE PAWS THAT REFRESHES"

WALKADOG
DOG EXERCISE SERVICE

- REASONABLE RATES BY THE WEEK OR MONTH
- FRIENDLY, EXPERIENCED SERVICE
- AVAILABLE SIX DAYS A WEEK
- ALL BREEDS ACCEPTED (MUTTS TOO!)
- RECOMMENDED BY THE ROXBURY KENNEL CLUB
- FOR INFORMATION, CALL (417) 218-3491

ROBIN JOHNSON
214 CHESTNUT CIRCLE
ROXBURY, ILL · 31281

TRAVEL BY . . .

You have been hired to write an ad campaign for traveling by bus. The only directions given you were that you must use an animal in the ad and stress safety. How will your ad read? What animal will you choose? Be prepared to deliver your ad to the class.

A SPECIAL LUNCH

You have won a contest. The prize is to have lunch with any famous person of your choice. Whom will you choose? What questions will you ask? What do you hope to learn by talking to this person?

SAVE THE ANIMALS

Choose your favorite animal. Pretend you own the last six of these animals on earth. If your six animals die and do not reproduce, they will be extinct. Write a letter to the president stating what qualities these animals have that make them unique and important. Write up a plan for saving them, including a plea for government assistance. How much money will you need? What kind of help from other people will you want? Do you think money alone will prevent your animals from becoming extinct?

YOUR OWN PARTY!

You are put in charge of your own birthday party. You can spend $100 for food and other things you want for the party. Write a description of your party. What food will you buy? What games will you play? How many people will you invite? Where will you have the party? Tell all about the plans for the big birthday party.

THE MAGIC BOX

You have a magic box that measures six feet high, six feet wide, and six feet long. It will make an exact copy of anything that is put in the box every five minutes. The magic of the box will last exactly ten days. In those ten days, what will you duplicate? Write a story about what could happen.

18

THE TIME MACHINE

You have the opportunity to be in an experiment with a time machine. The imaginary invention can transport you to any period, past or future, and any place in history you wish to visit. You can choose the date and place you will visit for three days. Write a story about where you will go, what period of history you will witness, and how you will feel when you return.

A NEW ONE

All animals seem to offer valuable lessons to people. Pretend you are a scientist and you have just created a new and unique animal. Describe the way it lives its life, the way it looks, and any other characteristics it might have. Draw a picture of it. What valuable lesson could your animal teach to people?

TEACHER TIME

Suppose your teacher is leaving to teach at a new school. The principal has given you and some friends the opportunity to interview some applicants for the job. Make a list of questions you will ask each applicant. Also make a list of qualities you will be watching for when talking to each person.

Name of applicant:

Education:

Special interests:

Teaching experience:

TAKE TWO

Pretend you are the film editor for a movie thriller. Describe in detail the setting you will choose for your movie. Be sure to include the time of day, the surroundings, and the mood of your setting. Remember, you want to give your audience the feelings of fear and anxiety.

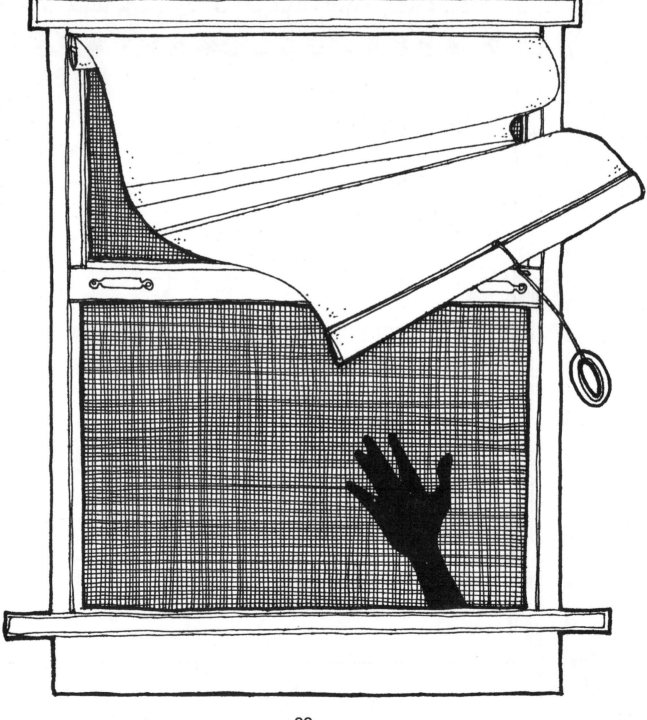

THE FAMILY

Sometimes we get an inaccurate idea of what the typical family is like from viewing television. Select a television program about a family. Watch the program and list what you think is realistic and unrealistic about the television family as compared to a "real" family. You may want to use your family as a comparison.

23

YOU'RE THE JUDGE

A family of four is fighting over the winnings of a lottery. Here are the facts: The son, age 9, had the idea to buy the ticket. The daughter, age 11, gave her brother the money to buy the ticket. The mother found the lottery ticket in the trash, and compared the number with the winning numbers in the newspaper. The father drove across town in less than ten minutes in order to claim the winnings before the deadline of the contest. Who should get the money? Why?

A DIFFICULT TEST

Mr. Jones, your teacher, is a very difficult grader. His tests are hard and often seem unfair. The night before the final test, a classmate calls to say he has a copy of the test. He invites you over to help him memorize the questions and answers. When you hesitate, he says you are chicken. What will you do?

A NEW FRIEND?

Pretend that a new person has moved next door to you during the summer vacation. You have discovered that this person frequently shoplifts. The day before school starts, your new neighbor says, "Let's walk to school together tomorrow." You do not want to keep up the friendship. Your neighbor is nervous about starting a new school, and wants your support. What will you do?

YOU CAN HELP

Your best friend has just started smoking. Your friend says it is because of a new ad campaign that shows young people smoking and having fun, and also because smoking is "in" with a certain group of classmates. You are concerned about your friend's health, and want to help her stop smoking. You know she will believe anything you tell her because you are best friends. Prepare your argument against smoking carefully.

TO GO OR NOT TO GO

When you get home from school you find your parents are quarreling. Your father has received a promotion, and his new job is on the other side of the country. He is excited about the move, his new and important position, and the increase in his salary. Your mother says she is not leaving the town you live in. Her mother is old and alone, and depends on your mother for help. The only solution seems to be for your parents to live apart. You want to live together as a family, and you feel that you are the only one who can convince your parents to change their minds. Who will you talk to and what will you say? What are your feelings about where **you** would live, having to choose?

DEAR EDITOR

Most people have something on their minds that really bothers them. A letter to the editor of a newspaper or magazine is one way of expressing a complaint. Think carefully about something you would like to see changed. Write a letter to the editor stating the problem and your idea for a solution. After you write your letter, you might want to send it to your local newspaper.

STAYING ALIVE

You have just spent six days backpacking deep into the woods. You pitch camp near a small water hole. You and a friend awaken the first morning to discover a bear has eaten all your food, ripped your backpacks apart, and destroyed your water containers and compass. You and your friend must plan for your survival. What will you do?

A DIFFERENT POINT OF VIEW

Pretend you have a little brother or sister who is extremely cruel to his or her pet. You have mentioned this to your parents, but they don't seem to want to deal with the problem. Pretend you are the pet. Write a story explaining how you feel.

FABLE FOR MOM

A fable is an animal story with a moral. Suppose you want to give your mother some advice, but you know she will not listen to you. She does, however, love to read your stories and might learn from a fable you write. What advice do you want to give your mother? Write a fable that teaches that lesson.

NEW PARENTS

Pretend a couple you know have adopted a teenager. They have asked you for help because they don't know much about teenagers, and would like to learn more. Make a list of do's and don'ts for the new parents. Be realistic in making your list.

IF I WERE ONLY YOUR AGE

How many times have you heard an adult say, "If I were only your age again"? Write a letter to someone who is always saying that. Tell them why it isn't always so easy to be your age. Tell them why they have advantages being the age they are.

THE PERFECT LIFE

Most people spend some time thinking about what they need to make them perfectly happy. Write a description of what you think would be the perfect life.

35

A TIMELY CHOICE

You are in charge of selecting the items that will go into a time capsule to represent this period of time. In 1,000 years the capsule is to be opened. You want to give a sample of life the way it is today. Choose your items carefully. Make a list of what you will put into the time capsule.

A LOOK INSIDE

It is the year 2500. Astronauts have intercepted a probe satellite from a civilization located in another galaxy. List the kinds of things you think the astronauts will find in the satellite. From your list, tell what you think the civilization is like.

THE BET

You have made a bet that you can outrun another person. The race has been going on for hours. You are at the end of your strength. You feel your opponent is indeed the stronger person. Write a story about how you originally got yourself into this position. Tell about the things you thought during the race. Tell about the final moments of the race and how it ended.

A BETTER TIME

Choose an age older or younger than you are now. Write a poem or story telling why you would like to be that age.

Name _____

AN INVENTION

Nearly everyone dreams of inventing something new. But people seldom put their ideas to work. Begin by writing a description of your invention. Give a detailed description of how it is built, what it does, and how it would be valuable to people. A drawing of your invention might be a good place to begin.

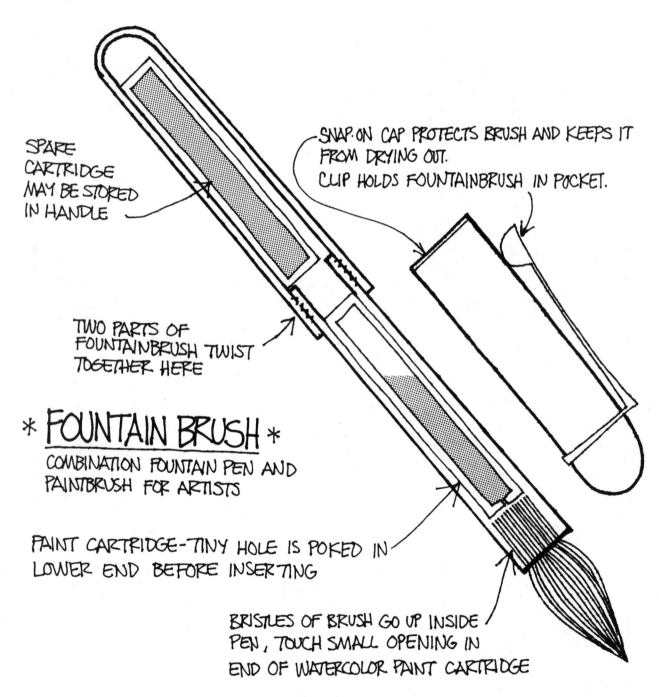

SPARE CARTRIDGE MAY BE STORED IN HANDLE

SNAP-ON CAP PROTECTS BRUSH AND KEEPS IT FROM DRYING OUT.
CLIP HOLDS FOUNTAINBRUSH IN POCKET.

TWO PARTS OF FOUNTAINBRUSH TWIST TOGETHER HERE

* FOUNTAIN BRUSH *
COMBINATION FOUNTAIN PEN AND PAINTBRUSH FOR ARTISTS

PAINT CARTRIDGE - TINY HOLE IS POKED IN LOWER END BEFORE INSERTING

BRISTLES OF BRUSH GO UP INSIDE PEN, TOUCH SMALL OPENING IN END OF WATERCOLOR PAINT CARTRIDGE

AN INTERESTING CHARACTER

Think of an interesting person you know and admire. Try to paint a picture of this person with words. Don't name the person you are writing about. When you are done with the character analysis, ask a friend to read your sketch.   See if your friend can name the person by reading the description of the character.

There aren't many people like him. He has had pet rattlesnakes, worked in the Pentagon, built a crossbow, and learned to speak (yes, speak) Morse code. He knows a lot of Indian lore: he can do beadwork and sand painting, and make arrowheads. He's a botanist: in college, instead of "wasting" money on cafeteria food, he ate edible plants growing on the campus. He knows and teaches survival skills: he can start a fire with flint and steel in less than five seconds. He plays guitar, recorder and piano. A magazine article about him said," He seems to know every verse to every song that was ever written." He knows sign language and karate, was a member of Mensa, and can carve rings out of peach pits.

In elementary school, he corrected a teacher's spelling. He won a district spelling bee, and they misspelled his name on the trophy. In high school, he and his friends designed and built rockets that flew several hundred feet. He is now head locksmith for a major aircraft corporation. Who IS this character?

DIFFERENT VIEWPOINTS

Write three paragraphs describing the same person. This person could even be **you**! The first paragraph should be a description of this person as seen by his or her parents. The second paragraph should be written from an enemy's point of view. The last paragraph should describe how the person sees himself or herself.

PARACHUTE

The parachute was invented to save lives. But remember, someone had to be the first to try it out. Pretend you have just invented the parachute. You are testing your own invention. Write a detailed account of your thoughts before the jump, during the test jump, and after you touch ground. Make your answer interesting for someone else to read.

Name _____

DOLPHINS

It is the year 2000. Using computers, scientists have managed to decode the language of the dolphins, and they have discovered that dolphins may be more intelligent than people. What would you ask the dolphins? What lessons will they have to offer people?

WONDER DRUG

A new wonder drug has been discovered. When it is taken, the aging of the body stops. Would you take the drug? If you decide to take the drug, at what age would you choose to stop your aging process? Why did you choose this age?

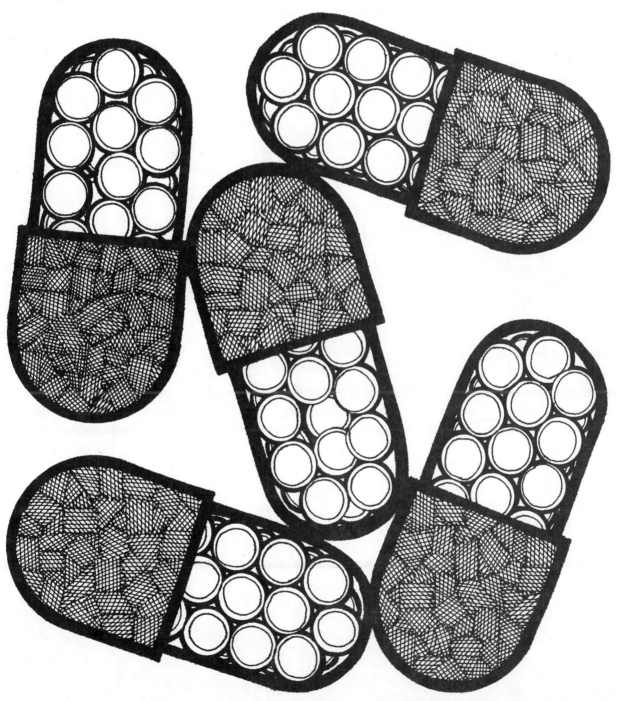

GRAND PRIZE

You have entered a contest, and, much to your amazement, you are chosen as the winner. The prize is a trip for you and a special friend to go anywhere in the world. Who will you take? Where will you go? What language will be spoken? What exciting sights and activities await you at your destination? What will you take? What will you want to buy to take home to remember your trip?

DESIGN TIME

Managers of Disneyland have asked you for ideas to add a new land to their amusement park. What will the new land be called? What kind of new rides will it have? What kind of theme will the land have? Draw pictures and write a description of your ideas.

47

CRYSTAL BALL

Some people are said to be psychic and can predict the future. Just for fun, make a list of ten predictions that you think might happen in the next five years.